Discovering the ~~C~~ 's

POWE ~~R P~~ AGES

Developed & Written by Carl Holden

Table of Contents

Introduction

You own your website.

Though Facebook or other trends may change, your website is the only part of your digital marketing that you have full control over. In a world of increasing ad costs, dropping social organic reach, or expanding competition, your site should be your most valuable and reliable asset. The best way to optimize this asset is through understanding your visitors and the data they leave behind. No tool is more capable of doing that than Google Analytics.

Analytics has a great training program, which I do suggest you take. It's obviously made by engineers and focuses heavily on data functions. I run a marketing company, so I know all your burning questions are not answered in their training. What data really matters? How do I make marketing decisions from all of this? What do I use and what can I ignore? Where do I even start?

The Power Pages

A Google Analytics account has over 100 different pages of data. The Power Pages are 15 different pages in Google Analytics that contain the most valuable data for a majority of marketing efforts. This is not a comprehensive and exhaustive instruction manual, rather it is a highlight reel to help you save time and optimize your research and monitoring efforts.

I will go over a few additional features such as some basics on installation and administration. These are basic skills that will assist you in wielding the Power of Analytics.

Once you understand the individual data contributions to your marketing, you can begin a process called the Power Pages Analytics Cycle. This process will help you consistently use Analytics to drive better conversions in your website through all your marketing activities.

We will review the Cycle at the end once we cover each individual Power Page. You will then see how to use Analytics to increase your most important website metric, conversions.

Conversions

The true power of Analytics is creating Conversions, which are desired actions tracked on your website. Once you understand that fact, you can begin to understand what makes these Power Pages. This is the end result of the Cycle. As you repeat the Cycle you will continue to improve your results.

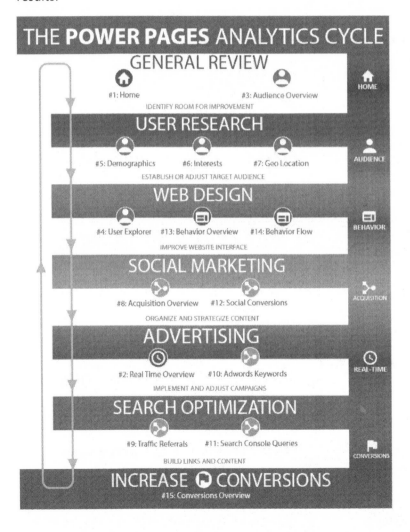

Installation

Start a Google Analytics Account.

Starting an account is easy. It must be done with a Google hosted email. If you are doing this for a company, make sure the account is one that will be permanent. Avoid starting Analytics on personal Gmails and definitely avoid having a third party start one for you. If you hired a marketing company to do your website and Analytics, make sure that you own the account that the Analytics was created on.

This is the link to start an account. Fill out the prompts. Most are self-explanatory.

https://analytics.google.com/analytics/web/

Place the Code.

At the end of your account creation, Analytics will show you how to install the code on your site. Every website page has a header section that loads before the rest of the page. You'll place the Analytics code into the HTML code of your header.

Analytics will also show you a unique tracking ID that looks something like this:

UA-1234567-89

Depending on what your website was designed with, you either place the tracking ID or the entire tracking code. For website builders like Squarespace, you only need the ID number (they place the ID into the code for you). Often you can find this in administration or settings section.

If you are running a WordPress, you will need to install a plugin to place the code. There are several Google Analytics plugins, but I've found most of those to be unreliable and some even stop recording data if they get out of date.

The best solution is to install a plugin that lets you copy and paste code directly into your header section. The following is a reliable plugin. Just copy the tracking code and paste it into the header section of the plugin once installed.

https://wordpress.org/plugins/insert-headers-and-footers/

Test if it is working.

The best way to know if you did it right is to go to the Real Time tab on the Reports section. If you don't know how to get there, just keep reading. If you do, go to that tab, and then load up your website on your computer and phone. If you see that two users are on your website (the computer and the phone), it is working properly.

Wait.

If your account is completely new, you're going to have to let time pass for it to collect data. Analytics does not have access to any previous data, it only starts tracking data from the time it is installed on the site.

Obtaining a Demo Account

Google Merchandise Store

Besides looking at your own data, a great way to become acquainted with the software is to look at a website that has large data sets for a long time. Google sells real merchandise on an online store. They use their merchandise site as a real sample account for Google Analytics.

You can gain access to this account by going to

https://support.google.com/analytics/answer/6367342

ACCESS DEMO ACCOUNT ☑

Click this button:

If you already have an Analytics account, it will place this Merch Store in your list of website properties. You will immediately start viewing the data. If you don't have an account, it will help you set one up.

Several screenshots and examples in this book will come from this account. I highly suggest using the demo to get the most out of this book. Feel free to pause your read and look at each page I will describe.

Google Analytics Interface

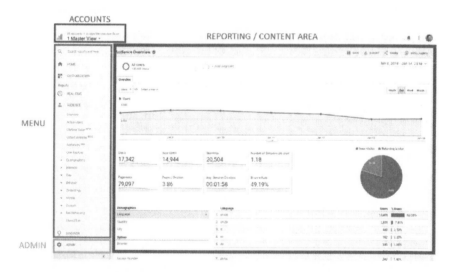

Accounts

This top left button allows you to switch between any of the Analytics accounts that you own. It also lets you switch between different Views (or separate versions) of the same account.

Menu

You will find 90% of the information you need by navigating this tabbed section. This is the portal to access the Power Pages, as well as all other pages of Analytics.

Admin

A part of the menu, the admin section is exactly what is sounds like. From here you can administrate actions such as adding new users, adding IP filters or creating conversion events.

Reporting/Content Area

Every time you select a tab from the Menu, this section will reflect the data you seek.

[The colors in the illustration are for separation purposes and do not correlate with Power Pages.]

Power Pages Overview

There are a lot of tabs in Google Analytics, but we are going to cover only these pages. They contain powerful sets of data but feel free to use more pages than these if you so choose.

Color coding: The six colors purple, red, blue, orange, pink, and green are unique to this book and do not exist like this in Analytics. Their assigned color is to help you visually separate where a page comes from and then organize them within the Cycle.

HOME

REAL-TIME

    Overview

AUDIENCE

    Overview | User Explorer | Demographics | Interests |
Geo

ACQUISITION

    Overview | All Traffic | AdWords | Search Console |
Social

BEHAVIOR

    Overview | Behavior Flow

CONVERSIONS

    Goals

I will explain why each page is powerful and why you should utilize it on a regular basis.

Terminology

There are many elements in Analytics. These definitions will help you better understand the reports.

- **User** is a visitor who has had at least one Session.
- **Session** is a period of time that one user is engaged.
- **Pageviews** is page views by all Users and their Sessions.
- A **Bounce** is a single-page Session. A Bounce Rate is how many sessions only had one page view. 100% is bad. 60% or less is good.
- A **Goal** is a specific action that you designate as a conversion.
- **Source** refers to where the traffic of your website came from. There are many sources:
  - **Organic Search**—Visitors who come to your website after searching Google.com and other search engines
  - **Paid Search**—Visitors who come to your website from an AdWords or other paid search ad
  - **Direct**—Visitors who come to your website without a traceable referral source, such as typing your URL into their address bar or using a bookmark on their browser
  - **Social**—Visitors who come to your website from a social network
  - **Referral**—Visitors who come to your website from another website by clicking on a link; Some ads may fall into this category if they are not identified properly
  - **Other**—If you use custom parameters for custom campaign tracking, the traffic linked to those campaigns is listed here
  - **Affiliate**—If you have affiliate programs, there's a way to track it via this metric
  - **Display**—Banner or flash ad traffic

The Power of the Pages is Conversions

A conversion is a **completed action on a website**, which could be buying a product, signing up for a newsletter, registering for a webinar, downloading a whitepaper, or filling out a contact form. There are many other conversions, but these are common examples.

Whenever someone has completed one of these actions on your website, Analytics can count it as a "conversion." We will go over how to set up conversions via Goals later in this book.

Website traffic is great for companies like Buzzfeed or the Huffington Post, but most businesses do not make money from ad revenue. Even those companies would like conversions such as email sign ups or premium memberships.

Traffic is fickle and hard to organize and monetize. Every website really needs conversions: actions of users that are expressing real interest or intent.

Let's say one in every 500 visitors becomes a customer while one in every five form submissions becomes a customer. If your goal is to double sales, would you want 20 form completions or 1000 new visitors? One thousand visitors would only result in two customers while 20 form submissions are four customers. It's easier to convert the traffic you already have than it is to get new traffic.

Google Analytics mainly tracks conversions by URL destinations. If you fill out a form, Analytics can mark the "/thank-you" page as a conversion. If you order an online item, Analytics can mark the "/order-review" page as a conversion. The ending page is the easiest way to signal they have completed an action you desire. By using a bit of code, you can also count button clicks, video views, and other actions as conversions.

The Power Pages highlight important data when deciding how to optimize your website conversions. Once you understand their signals and signs, you can begin to mold your website into a conversion machine.

SECTION 1: Home

 HOME

Power Page #1: Home

There are over 100 pages you can access in Analytics. The Power Pages will show you the most pertinent data to accomplishing your goal of converting traffic into customers.

The power of this page is its ability to save time. There are several important data graphs on this page. You can check up on your general website progress and have a top-level idea of performance. Again, most of the screenshots will be coming from the Google Merchandise store.

The Home page contains at least one important graph from each of the other five main sections of Analytics. Most have a link in the bottom right of the section to view that page. They also contain time controls on the bottom left, allowing you to quickly view progress over multiple periods of time.

If you have only 5 minutes to check up on your account, this is the page to visit. If you are reporting general data to a client or boss, this is the perfect page to obtain an overview.

The top right contains this button:

This button is found on many other pages but is very applicable to this page. You can ask it questions and it will give answers according to the data. It's not perfect, but you can learn a lot without ever leaving the Home page.

Unfortunately, you cannot customize which reports show up on Home as Google chooses what goes on it. If you are tracking ecommerce like this website, it shows additional sales graphs.

Speaking of customization, why am I not including the Customization page as a Power Page? It is located right underneath the Home page tab.

For large companies with teams devoted to data, this is indeed a Power Page. You're probably fine to skip this section for now. If you become skilled with Analytics or if you are a data scientist, this section would be good to learn. For the average user, most of the data you need is found in the other pages without any customization.

SECTION 2: Real-time

 REAL-TIME

Power Page #2: Real Time Overview

It is fascinating to see live data. It shows you real human beings who are looking at your website right now.

What can anonymous users on your site really tell you? Most of the important data you will view on Analytics is after that user has already completed their session.

If you are running an ad on social or online and you want to know if it is driving people NOW, this is how you can tell. So, if you're working for a large company spending a lot on social media or video ads, this is a good place to view how they are working.

If you want to see if a TV ad is driving website traffic, get on your Real Time page and watch. If you are wondering if guesting on a webinar is bringing you visitors, you can see them in real time.

That's the Power of Real Time – checking if a live activity is really working, especially those whose origins are harder to track (such as television and radio). Don't be surprised if they don't work as well as you hoped. They are indeed a dying art.

While it is great to confirm the users are present, the data they leave behind is more useful.

There's far more to Real Time than just the Overview page. Feel free to look at subpages if you want.

SECTION 3: Audience

 AUDIENCE

Power Page #3: Audience Overview

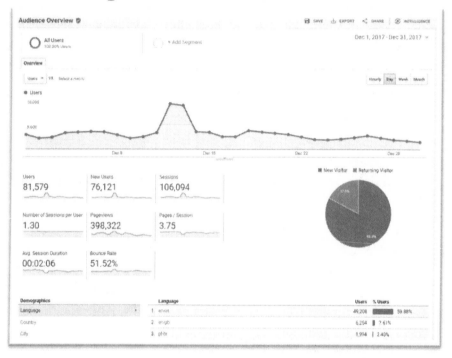

If you need a page to review general traffic numbers, look no further than the Audience Overview. It can quickly tell you the number of users, how many views, how many average pages per session, how long the user stays, and more.

This is also a great page to spot spikes in traffic as you can see in the visual.

Most pages come with a date range found near the top right of the page.

By selecting a second date range you can compare previous periods of time to see if your traffic quality has improved or if a spike is abnormal. As we can see below, the spike in December is definitely not normal. We can also see that while we obtained more users, the quality of their visits dropped.

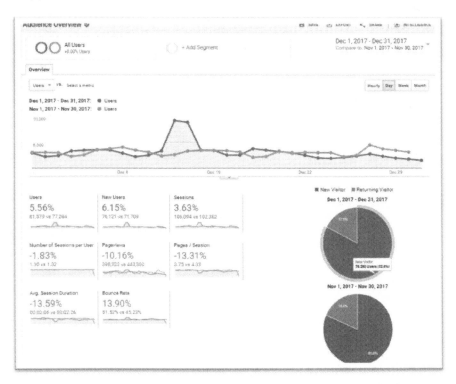

The Power of this Page is to understand how your traffic fluctuates and to determine the quality of the traffic. As the word denotes, your Audience are the people (users) viewing your site. You can compare your traffic numbers against your marketing activities to produce correlations. Traffic spiked on the 12th and 13th with the Audience, but we will need more data. Negatively, we also saw slight decreases in traffic quality. Once you identify these abnormalities, you can use other Power Pages to discover why the change may have occurred.

Power Page #4: User Explorer

Through this page, you can look at any individual who comes to your site, tracking exactly what they did and when they did it. This is a great way to research how people interact with your site, especially those who complete a conversion.

Unlike the rest of Google Analytics, this page focuses on individual users rather than averaging users' collective behavior. While they remain anonymous, you get a peek into how each person navigates your site.

In this example, a user buys a Google backpack and then checks on his order a few times each day. Google could use this specific case to make marketing decisions. Instead of just showing his order on this page, they should give him a coupon or deal on this page as an incentive for placing another order, since he was faithfully checking it each day.

The Power of this Page is in the individual. Pay close attention to those who convert. Investigate what they did before conversion and afterward. Pull up your site and try to mimic what the user did. You will invariably learn something, and this activity can lead to ideas.

Power Page #5: Demographics

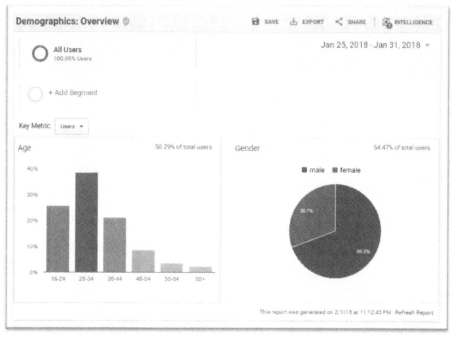

This one is simple. Google will tell you the age and gender of your users. Compare this data against the customer you are currently seeking. The average Google Merchandise store visitor is male, 25-34 years of age. Under Demographics Overview are specific pages for both age and gender.

If you run an ad for 45-54 year olds on Facebook for a week, this is a great place to see if it worked. Each individual page also allows you to compare that demographic with a secondary metric. Believe it or not, ages 45-54 consistently outperformed 18-24 in conversion rate throughout most of 2017 on the Merch store. While there were fewer in the older age group, Google could experiment to see if greater advertising to this group could produce a higher overall conversion rate.

The Power of this Page, and the data from its subpages, is to check your marketing personas against the actual traffic. Does your audience match your expectation? Does an age group or gender perform better/worse than expected? Using this data, how should your market targeting change to improve your conversions?

Power Page #6: Interests

Many ignore the great marketing potential that this Page and its subpages can offer. First, it's important to note that you may need an active AdWords account to access this data. It is recording other ads this user has clicked on to give you data on what his interests are.

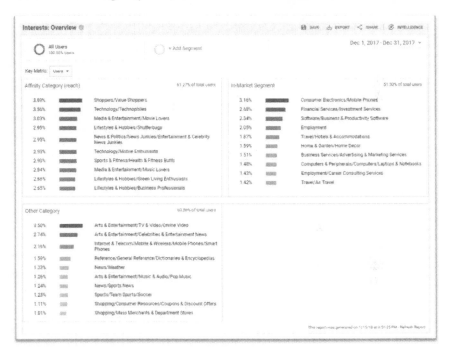

There are three main groups. You can click the group name to see the entire list of interests.

Affinity analyzes someone's overall interests, passions, and lifestyle to get a better sense of their overall identity.

In-Market tells you what industry-related products and services your users want, giving you even more ideas about how to improve the content of your site or other marketing efforts. These show you their potential purchase intent, giving you insight into what they are interested in buying while visiting you.

Other categories show you less-related affinities that your visitors show.

The Power in this Page is that it's pure market research! It shows you what interests the people in your market. Looking for marketing ideas? Topics for blog posts? Who you should be seeking out as industry partners? This page can reveal that information to you. It's more honest than any survey your users would take because search history can't lie.

Power Page #7: Geo Location

The fact is, everyone will get useless traffic, no matter how big or small your site is. If you want to tell if actual residents of your area are visiting, the Geo > Location tab shows you how much of your traffic is located in the desired geographic market.

If you are a local business, traffic from a state across the U.S. is not valuable. You want to focus on your core market and on improving web traffic from that market.

This is a screenshot from a client of mine, a home builder headquartered in Huntsville, Alabama. One month they got 7525 Sessions. Only 64% of it (4869 sessions) was in Alabama. This company should focus on growing the localized traffic, not overall numbers.

The Power of this page is to understand what traffic really matters by paying attention to location. Make goals and track your progress with location in mind. Interestingly, the city in which the home builder company had the highest conversion rate is Toney and not their home city of Huntsville. Use this data to decide where advertising should occur.

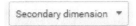

You can use the secondary dimension tool to then compare other demographics, such as age or traffic source.

SECTION 4: Acquisition

 ACQUISITION

Acquisition is all about where your users came from. Helpful to fully understanding this data, definitions for each source are important. These were defined previously, but it will not hurt to review them again.

Organic Search—Visitors who come to your website after searching Google.com and other search engines

Paid Search—Visitors who come to your website from an AdWords or other paid search ad

Direct—Visitors who come to your website without a traceable referral source, such as typing your URL into their address bar or using a bookmark on their browser

Social—Visitors who come to your website from a social network

Referral—Visitors who come to your website from another website by clicking on a link; Some ads may fall into this category

Other—If you use custom parameters for custom campaign tracking, the traffic linked to those campaigns is listed here

Affiliate— If you have affiliate programs, there's a way to track it via this metric

Display—Banner or flash ads

Power Page #8: Acquisition Overview

All Section Overview pages are Power Pages. Check them frequently.

From this page we can see traffic sources, which types of traffic produced quality visits, and which traffic created the most conversions. This screenshot shows that Referral traffic had the highest conversion rate. You could then click Referral to view which links were driving this conversion behavior.

The Power in this Page is that it's a clear indicator of the results of your marketing. By attaching conversions to your online marketing activities, you can justify actions or recommend revisions. It will easily tell you what marketing activities are effective and what you need to work on improving.

Remember Power Page #3, Audience Overview? There was a big spike in traffic on December 12th and 13th. By using Acquisition and narrowing down the date range, we can see what caused this spike in traffic. We find that Direct traffic drove most of it but unfortunately that Direct traffic did not drive very many conversions. If you then consult Geo, you will find most of this Direct traffic came from Google Headquarters in California.

Compare your marketing calendar and activities with this data. Use correlation to decide how to improve these activities. Repeat and remix the activities that yielded quality results.

Power Page #9: Traffic Referrals

It's important to focus on what websites provide traffic and hopefully conversions on your site. Google will always value this traffic highly for

SEO purposes. Discovering the source of this traffic and increasing the links that drive conversions will improve your website goals.

Google, of course, has plenty of links around the web so I clicked one from Business Insider. As you can see, links from two articles on businessinsider.com drove over 50 users who had a relatively low bounce rate. While they did not buy anything, this was good traffic. If Google were a smaller business, I would advise them to work with Business Insider on a more regular basis.

The Power of the page is that referral links tend to have a low bounce rate and moderate conversion potential. Work on a marketing strategy that will optimize these existing links and contact the website moderators to foster partnerships in the future.

Power Page #10: AdWords Keywords

Many modern marketing strategies include Google advertising, especially if your website is not appearing organically at the top of Google searches. AdWords is a robust platform. Given its complexity, we will not be talking about its functions inside of this book.

Keep in mind that your AdWords account will let you bid on words and then track how many clicks you received. It can even track conversions if you set them up in the platform. To make a truly informed decision about which ads to buy, connect the two platforms. This can be done on the Admin page under Product Linking.

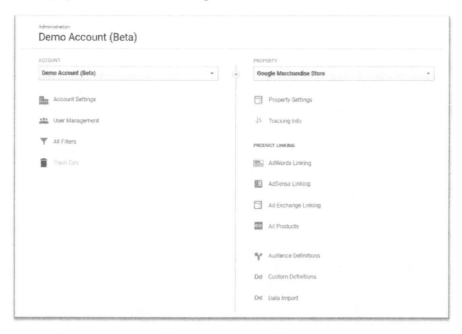

If you need any help, these are the instructions:https://support.google.com/analytics/answer/1033961?hl=en

While there are many pages to view, Keywords is the most actionable data. This is a screenshot from a client of mine. I don't actually run their AdWords, but I do advise them occasionally on the account.

If they needed to drop one keyword in this list, which one should it be?

Keyword	Clicks ↓	Cost	CPC	Sessions	Bounce Rate	Pages / Session	Available Homes (Goal 1 Conversion Rate)	Available Homes (Goal 1 Completions)
	13,939 % of Total 100.00% (13,939)	$7,752.86 % of Total 100.00% ($7,752.86)	$0.56 Avg for View: $0.56 (0.00%)	15,221 % of Total: 19.33% (78,887)	40.86% Avg for View: 41.85% (-1.91%)	4.07 Avg for View: 4.24 (-4.04%)	22.20% Avg for View: 17.86% (24.28%)	3,379 % of Total: 24.09% (14,028)
1. new homes in madison al	938 (6.73%)	$554.99 (7.16%)	$0.59	1,056 (6.94%)	30.21%	4.78	28.88%	305 (9.02%)
2. new homes in huntsville al	825 (5.92%)	$449.07 (5.79%)	$0.54	932 (6.12%)	30.26%	4.79	25.21%	235 (6.95%)
3. home for sale in huntsville al	742 (5.32%)	$500.64 (6.46%)	$0.67	649 (4.26%)	61.17%	2.51	20.96%	136 (4.02%)
4. homes in madison al	705 (5.06%)	$458.01 (5.91%)	$0.65	665 (4.37%)	51.43%	3.08	22.26%	148 (4.38%)
5. new homes huntsville	550 (3.95%)	$279.74 (3.61%)	$0.51	666 (4.38%)	30.18%	4.76	22.52%	150 (4.44%)
6. ▇▇▇▇ homes huntsville al	510 (3.66%)	$134.57 (1.74%)	$0.26	717 (4.71%)	25.94%	5.26	21.06%	151 (4.47%)
7. huntsville homes for sale	448 (3.21%)	$288.90 (3.73%)	$0.64	353 (2.32%)	61.47%	2.83	20.68%	73 (2.16%)
8. homes in huntsville al	440 (3.16%)	$274.47 (3.54%)	$0.62	405 (2.66%)	53.58%	2.90	21.98%	89 (2.63%)
9. homes for sale harvest al	429 (3.08%)	$276.75 (3.57%)	$0.65	414 (2.72%)	64.25%	2.25	20.77%	86 (2.55%)
10. homes for sale new market al	411 (2.95%)	$251.15 (3.24%)	$0.61	387 (2.54%)	66.15%	2.34	19.12%	74 (2.19%)

I would advise them to drop "home for sale in Huntsville al." First of all, they are a home *builder*—they don't sell existing homes. And that keyword may be used by people looking for existing homes as well. Also, the cost of that keyword is the highest and the bounce rate and pages per session are not great. If you were looking to funnel your budget into more effective keywords, dropping this keyword would be a great way to free up spend.

The Power of this Page is it lets you compare your AdWords campaign with your website goals. Advertising can be an important part of creating conversions. Use this page to rid your current list of underperforming keywords and focus on the words that are most effective in producing conversions.

Power Page #11: Search Console Queries

You can also connect your analytics account to your Search Console (aka Webmasters Account). While it doesn't offer near as much information as AdWords, this is important data you can review on an occasional basis.

Search Query	Clicks	Impressions	CTR	Average Position
	23,353 % of Total: 100.00% (23,353)	**1,619,433** % of Total: 100.00% (1,619,433)	**1.44%** Avg for View: 1.44% (0.00%)	**14** Avg for View: 14 (0.00%)
1. (other)	**6,372** (27.29%)	135,229 (8.35%)	4.71%	20
2. youtube merchandise	**1,437** (6.15%)	4,611 (0.28%)	31.16%	1.0
3. youtube merch	**1,063** (4.55%)	5,323 (0.33%)	19.97%	1.8
4. youtube shop	**887** (3.80%)	1,968 (0.12%)	45.07%	1.0
5. youtube store	**643** (2.75%)	1,420 (0.09%)	45.28%	1.0
6. google store	**501** (2.15%)	319,894 (19.75%)	0.16%	6.9
7. google electronics	**448** (1.92%)	2,451 (0.15%)	18.28%	1.2
8. google t shirt	**437** (1.87%)	1,677 (0.10%)	26.06%	1.0
9. google shop	**416** (1.78%)	46,778 (2.89%)	0.89%	6.5
10. google merchandise store	**364** (1.56%)	6,463 (0.40%)	5.63%	1.0

I don't have a legitimate answer on why Google lumps most searches into an unknowable "(other)". Why bother showing that at all? There are even some videos out there of Google employees dodging the question.

If you are looking to grow traffic and conversions via SEO, the metrics above are important for determining your search optimization priorities.

From the list above, I would say their best performing query is "YouTube store" because it is number one with the highest CTR. People obviously have found what they are looking for with that search query. To best improve organic traffic rates, improve the ranking of words that have a high CTR.

The Power of this Page is to monitor and adjust your SEO focus when it comes to organic ranking in Google. This is also a great page to show clients or bosses to prove that conversions on your website are directly related to your SEO efforts.

Power Page #12: Social Conversions

A constant question for marketers: "Is my social media marketing making a difference?" This is the page that will tell you that.

Much of social media should be viewed as awareness campaigning. Every post will not convert your followers into customers. If you view the Conversions Overview tab of the Google site, you will see that even a large company like Google has only a small part of its conversions coming from social media.

The important page is the tab underneath Overview, labeled Conversions. You can view a list of all your social presence and the amount of conversions they generate.

If you are struggling to justify the cost or time of running social media, this is a good place to view your return on investment. If all conversions are assigned a monetary value, you can see the ROI of the social efforts.

By clicking each social platform, you can view their individual daily conversions.

The Power of this Page is the ability to view conversions on each social account and compare that to your content for that space of time. This intelligence will help you make decisions about what content is most effective at generating conversions.

SECTION 5: Behavior

 BEHAVIOR

Behavior focuses on the traffic moving within the site rather than where the traffic came from or who the visitors are. Behavior is an important aspect in understanding the design and flow of your website.

Power Page #13: Behavior Overview

The data here is straightforward. It shows us the number of pages and time spent on the website. It is interesting to compare December (blue) to November (orange) for this Google store.

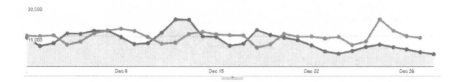

Just as you would expect, pageviews jump in the end of November and beginning of December and then taper off into the new year. That is surely holiday gift spending.

The Power of this Page is to keep a close eye on pageviews and make sure that recent changes in your website increase, not decrease, pageviews. The other powerful data here is the list of the most frequented pages. Your goal should be for your conversion-centered pages to be at the top of this list. If a page already receives a lot of traffic, you can also formulate a way to encourage conversions through that page as well.

Any time you are making major changes to the layout of your website, Behavior data should be consulted.

Power Page #14: Behavior Flow

This page charts how your users are flowing through the site. The red means they are leaving the website.

Google does not currently have heatmapping software in Analytics, so you must guess a bit on the reasons for their navigation. However, an important feature to point out is the green dropdown above the white boxes (top left). It defaults on Landing Pages as seen below. The one I prefer to change it to is Source, but you could also select other helpful categories such as AdWords Campaign or Social Network.

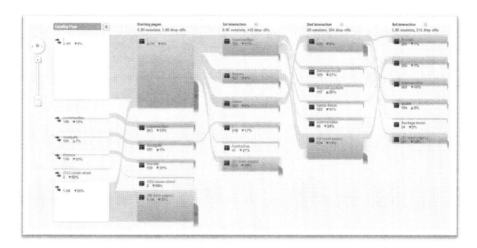

When you designate Source in the top left, you can see how Search traffic behaviors may differ from Social traffic behaviors. By clicking any individual box, you can highlight traffic just through that page.

The Power of this Page is reviewing the traffic flow from page to page. What pages have a high drop off? What page do visitors frequently go to next? How can I alter my site to shift their path towards pages that result in conversions?

SECTION 6: Conversions

 CONVERSIONS

TO REPEAT:

A conversion is a completed action on a website, which could be buying a product, signing up for a newsletter, registering for a webinar, downloading a whitepaper, or filling out a lead/contact form.

Whenever someone has completed one of these actions on your website, Analytics can count it as a "conversion."

You must always think about the intent of the user. When a user visits a valuable page, that could be counted as a conversion. But can you really measure how interested they are from a visit alone? By all means, track certain page visits if you think there's value. What you really need to track are actions.

The easiest conversion to track is a purchase. The identifiable URL that signals the conversion is the Thank You or Order Review page. They can't get there unless they completed a sale, which is of course a valuable conversion.

The most concrete conversion URLs are ones that visitors can't navigate to without performing an action. The page shouldn't exist in the menu or general navigation, so they must follow your conversion path.

Not every website is ecommerce. The next best way to track a conversion event is to use a URL redirect after they fill out a form, sending them to a page that says thanks.

Before we go over the pages that highlight your conversions, I'd like to quickly explain how conversions are set up.

First click the Admin button on the bottom left of the menu bar.

 ADMIN

You will then select Goals from under the current View. It's right under View Settings.

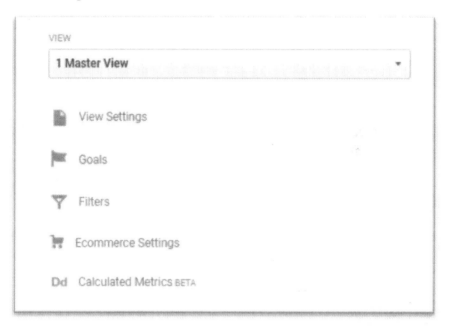

In the demo account, you will see that conversion Goals have already been created but will not allow you to create any. In your own account, you will also see a red button like this to create a Goal.

Google gives you a lot of options. I could write a whole book explaining each of these but that's not the purpose of this book. If you have a question about a specific one, you can usually find a tutorial on it if you Google "How to set up a _____ goal in analytics." Many of them are very similar but there are a few that have a unique setup. An easy one to use by default is the Contact Us form.

Step 2 then allows you to choose what signals the conversion. It can be a URL destination, a length of time on a page, a certain number of pages per session, or an event like watching a video. Again, an easy one to track is a URL destination.

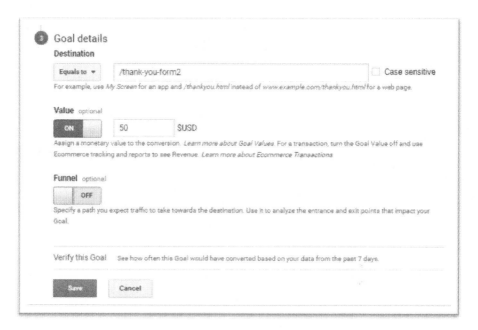

You then place the Destination URL into the first line. You can assign it a value, even if it's not a sale. This is a good way to weight the importance of your conversions in comparison to each other.

The funnel allows you to track if they visit a certain page before the conversion. This comes in handy if you have a preferred page or pages before they convert.

You can "Verify this Goal" to check if someone would have converted based on the existing data. This will not add backdated conversions.

Once you hit Save, the conversion Goal has been created. It's important to note that for whatever reason, Goals cannot be deleted. You can only create 20 Goals per View. If you have more Goals than that, just create a new View (which is basically a copy of the data). You can create up to 25 Views of a single Analytics-tracked website.

You will need to create these Goals and allow people to complete them before any data can be shown in the Conversion section.

Power Page #15: Conversions Overview

This is the hub to check your progress on Conversions. Your aim should be to improve your Goal Completions every month and keep a high Conversion Rate. You can also match this page to your social media or other marketing activities to help you understand which of your content is producing conversions.

Two additional pages that might be helpful are Goal URLs and Reverse Goal Path. Goal URLs are a longer list from the Overview page. Reverse Goal Path shows what URLs they visited before hitting your Goal. That's helpful if you don't have a set funnel and you want to see which pages they visit before converting.

The Power of the Page is Conversions! If you want the website to start showing more profitable results, use this page to consistently check your progress.

Utilizing the Power Pages

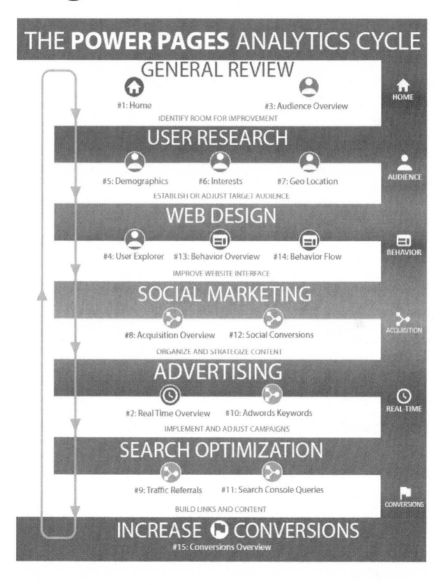

The power of this tool is it helps you see where Google Analytics can be implemented throughout your marketing campaign.

With this Cycle, you can evaluate your current marketing process against your website data. To review the usefulness of each page, consult the Table of Contents and select that Page to re-read. Here's how The Power Pages Analytics cycle may work for you.

GENERAL REVIEW

Using Power Page#1 and #3, review your website's progress compared to your previously reviewed period. Make note of increases in traffic and conversions and places for improvement. Check for any sudden spikes or drops in traffic.

USER RESEARCH

Reviewing data in Power Pages #5, #6, and #7, check if your audience has changed in comparison to the previously reviewed period. In your current period, evaluate if you are reaching the correct market in terms of age, gender and location. Use Interests to get content ideas for the site or other marketing efforts. This will establish important User Research.

WEB DESIGN

Using Page #4, identify a handful of users with optimal goals accomplished. Make note of their individual activities and plan how to encourage such interactions. Monitoring pages #13 and #14 will help you understand overall website flow and prompt potential interface changes to your site.

SOCIAL MARKETING

Pages #8 and #12 will reflect the efforts your social media work has had on driving traffic and conversions. Compare dates of high data against your content calendar to note what worked well. Focus on social interactions that resulted in conversions and how to repeat such success.

ADVERTISING

Page #2 will help if you have live ads running that should result in immediate traffic. Consult Page #10 to review your AdWords progress and how it is accomplishing your website goals. Adjust as necessary.

SEARCH OPTIMIZATION

Review #9 to see which acquired or earned links are driving traffic and conversions. Use #11 to check if your keyword ranking efforts are resulting in noticeable traffic increases.

INCREASE CONVERSIONS

Each of the previous activities should be conversion focused. Review all conversions and identify how and why they were acquired. Set marketing goals and tactics on how your upcoming activities will implement the knowledge learned from the data.

Repeat!

Google Analytics is a tool that should be on the top of your marketing toolbox. It helps you understand the most important data related to converting customers. Cycling through this table will keep your goals fresh and up to date and provides accountability and measurability. Regular review will foster improvement better than haphazard checking. It's a colorful chart but not always a glamorous endeavor. You rarely can acquire more useful data than this. I encourage you to implement this Cycle as a part of your process.

For a PDF download of The Power Pages Analytics Cycle, please visit my website theinvestmethod.com/analytics-cycle You can contact me for speaking engagements and consultation from that site.

Thanks for reading. Connect to me via social or email through that website. Good luck on your Analytics journey and may the Power Pages be your guide to higher website conversions!

Made in the USA
San Bernardino, CA
31 August 2018